A Child's Story of Easter

BY

Fulton Oursler

ILLUSTRATED BY HELEN CASWELL

A CHILD'S STORY OF EASTER
Copyright © 1951 by Fulton Oursler
Copyright © renewed 1978 by Fulton Oursler, Jr.,
Will Oursler, and April Armstrong.
Illustrations copyright © 1996 by Helen Caswell.

This book is printed on recycled, acid-free paper.
ISBN 0-687-02190-1
96 97 98 99 00 01 02 03 04 — 10 9 8 7 6 5 4 3 2 1
Manufactured in Mexico

Abingdon Press
Nashville

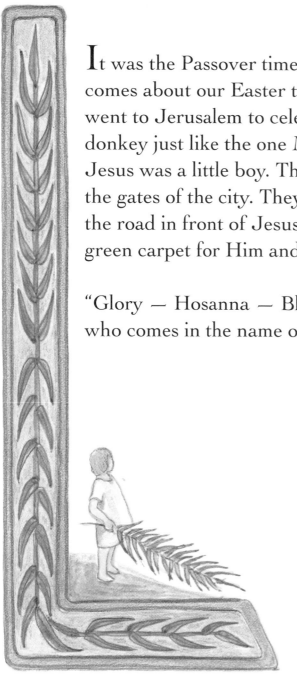

It was the Passover time. That is a great holiday, and comes about our Easter time. Jesus and His friends went to Jerusalem to celebrate. Jesus was riding on a donkey just like the one Mary and Joseph had when Jesus was a little boy. Thousands of people met Him at the gates of the city. They threw palm leaves down on the road in front of Jesus and the donkey to make a green carpet for Him and they sang to Him.

"Glory — Hosanna — Blessed is the King of Israel who comes in the name of the Lord."

The rulers of the country were worried. They said to themselves: "The people call Him king. The people love Him. Soon they will do only what He tells them and not what we tell them. We will have to kill this Jesus."

Jesus knew their cruel thoughts. He knew something even worse. He knew one of His own twelve friends would leave Him and help the cruel rulers kill him.

And at the same time, Jesus said: "I shall leave you but I shall return to you."

They did not know what He meant but later they found out.

On Thursday night, Jesus sent all twelve of His friends to the upper room of a house in Jerusalem. They sat there and waited for Him. While they waited for Him they talked and soon they had an argument. What do you suppose they were arguing about? Who would sit nearest Jesus! That was what each one wanted: to sit nearest to Jesus.

When Jesus opened the door and saw what a quarrel was going on He was sad. He took a bowl of water and a towel. One by one He washed the feet of each of the twelve. That was to show them how wrong it was to want to be greater than others. Jesus is the Son of God. He is truly God as well as truly human, but He washed the feet of His friends. The person who does the most to help others is nearest to the Son of God.

Then Jesus sat down at a long table. All the twelve sat with Him. This was their last supper together. Jesus told them they would never eat together again. His friends turned pale. Why did this have to be the last supper? What was going to happen?

Jesus told them He was going to be killed. Who would kill Him? Rulers in Jerusalem who were afraid of Him. They wanted to catch Him that night. But these rulers did not know where Jesus stayed at night. One of the twelve friends, Jesus said, would tell His enemies where to look for Him.

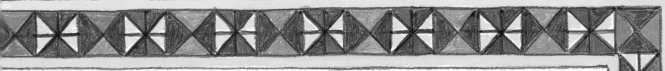

The friends began to ask:
  "Lord, is it I?"
  "Do you mean me?"
  "Who is it, Lord?"
  Judas was sitting with one hand on the table. And Jesus said: "The hand of him who will betray me is on the table."

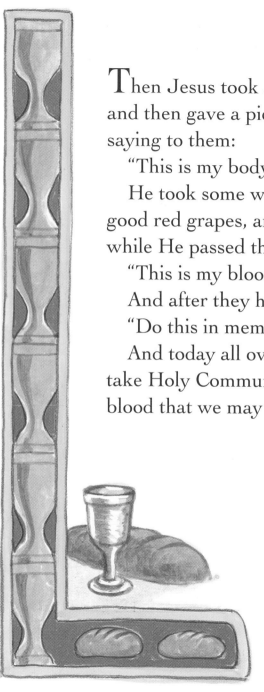

Then Jesus took a piece of bread and broke it. He prayed and then gave a piece of the bread to each of His friends, saying to them:

"This is my body. Take and eat."

He took some wine in a cup, wine made of the juice of good red grapes, and He blessed it and gave thanks to God while He passed the cup to His apostles and said:

"This is my blood. Drink this."

And after they had each taken a sip He said:

"Do this in memory of me."

And today all over the world those of us who love Him take Holy Communion, as it is called, receiving His body and blood that we may become one with the life of Jesus.

When the night was dark, Jesus asked His followers to come with Him to a garden of olive trees. It was called the Garden of Gethsemane. That was where He often spent the night.

It was too dark to see anything in the garden. The moon was not shining. How could the men who wanted to kill Him even find Him here? Jesus knelt down beside a big rock. Then He asked His friends to keep watch while He prayed. Then He talked to God. He knew that men were getting ready to kill Him. He asked God if God could stop the men from killing Him. But, He said, He would do whatever God wanted Him to. That was to show us all how to pray.

We ask God
for what we
would like to
have but tell God
we will give it up, and
forget about it, if God
does not think it is wise
for us to have our own
way.

While he was praying, Jesus heard a noise in the garden. He looked around. His friends were not watching. They were all asleep on the damp, cold grass. Only Jesus was awake. He saw lights near the garden gate. Soldiers were coming. Some carried burning staffs for lights. Others held long swords in their hands. But the man who led them all to Jesus had no sword and no light. He was Judas. He came up to Jesus and kissed Him.

That kiss was a signal to the soldiers. Now they knew which one to arrest. The soldiers grabbed Jesus. They made Him their prisoner. They tied His hands with cords. They marched Him to a cell and then tried Him in court.

He had many judges to hear His case. What had He done wrong? He had healed the sick. Was that wrong? No! He had made persons who were blind see. Was that wrong? No!

But He told people He was the Christ, the Son of God. The judges did not believe He was the Son of God.

So they said: "We will kill Him!"

But they could not kill Him right away. They had to go to a man called Pilate. He was the governor. Pilate did not want to kill Jesus, but the crowd of frightened people yelled so loudly that Pilate was scared, too. So he let them take Jesus away to kill Him.

They were cruel to Jesus now. They made a crown of thorns and put it on His head and the thorns cut His forehead and made Him bleed. They were making fun of Him because some people called Him their king. But Jesus was not a king of things. He was a king of the hearts of the people. They beat Jesus until He could hardly stand up. Then on Friday morning they nailed Him, hands and feet, to a big wooden cross. And they stood near to watch Him die.

Jesus, looking down from the cross, prayed for all of them, even for the men who killed Him:

"Forgive them, Father, for they do not know what they are doing."

Mary, His mother, loved Him more than ever for those wonderful words. Yes, poor Mary, the mother of Jesus, stood at the foot of the cross, and never took her eyes off of her beloved Son. She saw Him die.

Now all who loved Jesus were crying. They wrapped His body in a sheet and laid it in a little stone house called a tomb. They rolled a big stone against the door.

All Friday night and all day Saturday the stone lay fast against the door of the tomb. On Sunday morning some of His friends came to the tomb to pray. But look! How can this be? Something wonderful, something unbelievable has happened.

The stone is rolled away from the door of the tomb.
The tomb is empty.
The body is gone from the grave.
Where, then, is Jesus?
He is standing right here in the garden. Not dead, but living!
He has risen from the grave.

This Sunday, when Jesus rose from the dead, was the first Easter. That was when He proved what He had told the people: That if we love God and our neighbors, there is no death but life forever in Heaven with God and Jesus and the Holy Spirit.

For forty more days Jesus stayed on earth. Many times He visited with His friends. He told them He must go back to the Father in Heaven, but that no one who loved Him would ever be alone again:

"For I am with you always, even to the end of the world."

That is what He promised them the day He left the world and rose to be with His Father in Heaven.

And His promise of life forever was for you and for me and for everybody. That is the secret of the wonderful story of Jesus.

The wonderful Boy who was born in a stable came to earth to help people to be happy—not just the people who lived 2,000 years ago when He was born but all the people since then. The people today—you and I and the President and the toy store woman and the ice cream man and all the aunts and uncles and fathers and mothers and boys and girls today and tomorrow and always and always.

That is why the story is not finished yet. You and I can be a part of it if we know the secret, which is to let Jesus live in our hearts.

Each of us can help or hurt each other. Jesus wants us to help each other. Let us all try to live as Jesus taught.

If everyone were to love Jesus with the whole heart, how wonderful this world would be. No more greed or hate. No more war. Only peace—the peace that Jesus brings us from our Father in Heaven.